WRITER: Robert Kirkman
ARTIST: Sean Phillips
COLORIST: June Chung
LETTERER: VC's Rus Wooton
ASSISTANT EDITOR: Lauren Sankovitch
EDITOR: Bill Rosemann
SENIOR EDITOR: Ralph Macchio

COVER ARTIST: Arthur Suydam

COLLECTION EDITOR: Mark D. Beazley
ASSISTANT EDITORS: John Denning & Cory Levine
EDITOR, SPECIAL PROJECTS: Jennifer Grünwald
SENIOR EDITOR, SPECIAL PROJECTS: Jeff Youngquist
SENIOR VICE PRESIDENT OF SALES: David Gabriel
PRODUCTION: Jerry Kalinowski

EDITOR IN CHIEF: Joe Quesada
PUBLISHER: Dan Buckley

MARVEL ZOMBIES 2. Contains material originally published in magazine form as MARVEL ZOMBIES 2 #1-5. First printing 2008. ISBN# 978-0-7851-2545-7. Published by MARVEL PUBLISHING, INC., a subsidiary of MARVEL ENTERTAINMENT, INC. OFFICE OF PUBLICATION: 417 5th Avenue, New York, NY 10016. Copyright © 2007 and 2008 Marvel Characters, Inc. All rights reserved. $19.99 per copy in the U.S. and $21.00 in Canada (GST #R127032852); Canadian Agreement #40668537. All characters featured in this issue and the distinctive names and likenesses thereof, and all related indicia are trademarks of Marvel Characters, Inc. No similarity between any of the names, characters, persons, and/or institutions in this magazine with those of any living or dead person or institution is intended, and any such similarity which may exist is purely coincidental. **Printed in the U.S.A.** ALAN FINE, CEO Marvel Toys & Publishing Divisions and CMO Marvel Entertainment, Inc.; DAVID GABRIEL, SVP of Publishing Sales & Circulation; DAVID BOGART, SVP of Business Affairs & Talent Management; MICHAEL PASCIULLO, VP of Merchandising & Communications; JIM O'KEEFE, VP of Operations & Logistics; DAN CARR, Executive Director of Publishing Technology; JUSTIN F. GABRIE, Director of Editorial Operations; SUSAN CRESPI, Editorial Operations Manager; OMAR OTIEKU, Production Manager; STAN LEE, Chairman Emeritus. For information regarding advertising in Marvel Comics or on Marvel.com, please contact Mitch Dane, Advertising Director, at mdane@marvel.com. For Marvel subscription inquiries, please call 800-217-9158.

10 9 8 7 6 5 4 3 2 1

IT STARTED WITH A FLASH IN THE SKY, AND A RIPPLE THROUGH THE CLOUDS. THE HUNGER IS WHAT BROUGHT IT HERE — AND FEED IT DID, UNTIL THE MARVEL HEROES WERE NO MORE.

THEY WERE REPLACED BY SOULLESS MONSTERS, DRIVEN ONLY BY AN INSATIABLE HUNGER FOR HUMAN FLESH.

AFTER THEY RAN OUT OF FOOD, MISTER FANTASTIC DEVISED A PLAN TO LURE HIS COUNTERPART FROM ANOTHER DIMENSION INTO A DEADLY TRAP. THANKS TO MAGNETO, WHO HAD MANAGED TO STAY UNINFECTED, REED'S PLAN FAILED, LEAVING HIM AND THE REST OF THE FANTASTIC FOUR STRANDED IN ANOTHER DIMENSION.

MAGNETO HAS DESTROYED THE MACHINE THAT ALLOWED THEIR PASSAGE INTO ANOTHER DIMENSION — AN ACTION HE PAID FOR WITH HIS LIFE.

THE SILVER SURFER APPEARED IN THE SKIES FOLLOWED SHORTLY AFTER BY THE ARRIVAL OF GALACTUS. IT WAS LITTLE MORE THAN AN OBSTACLE FOR THE MONSTERS THE MARVEL HEROES HAD BECOME.

DEVOURING THE SILVER SURFER AND GALACTUS PROVIDED THE GHOULS WITH COSMIC POWERS AND COSMIC HUNGER. WITH NO FOOD LEFT ON EARTH, THEY SET THEIR SIGHTS FOR THE STARS, FOR SPACE — AND THE UNIVERSE WAS NEVER THE SAME AGAIN.

THIS IS NO WORLD OF MARVEL HEROES.

So that's it then? Nothing left?

Nothing?

It's been weeks--can't think--can't focus.

I don't think there's anything *left.*

The pain is *unbearable...* we've been moving through the cosmos--as fast as we can.

What now?!

We wouldn't *be* in this situation if *this* one didn't eat twice as much as the rest of us!

QUIET, PRUNE CHIN!!

Hulk not eat more than his fair share!

Prune Chin should shut up before Hulk forgets how bad he must taste!

Guk.

Stop it-- *both* of you!

Right now!

How many times do we have to tell you? We can't eat each other.

If only we could...

We're *done* here.

There's nothing to eat-- there's nothing left. We can't stay here.

We need to *leave.*

Yeah, bub--and go *where?* We've been *everywhere.*

Not everywhere. There was a machine, I remember it now, a way to get to other dimensions.

I remember...I think I remember working on that. Did I build it, before--before I was... dead?

Yes, and Reed Richards rebuilt it and used it to escape this dimension.

That's our ticket out of here-- that's our means of escape. That's how we get more *food.*

WE NEED TO GO BACK TO EARTH.

You ain't saying much. It's not like you. What gives?

Just thinking. I don't know...

It seems like the longer we go without eating, I could be imagining this but... it seems like the pain-- the *hunger* is, well...

...I think it's starting to *fade*.

Earth...

YEAAGH!!

Is someone there?! Someone? **Anyone?!**

Hello?!

Hold on--I'm coming.

≥gasp!≤

This is where I live.

Wow.

Damn it, T'Challa. There is far too much at stake for you to be so *casual* about this.

You need to start taking this threat seriously.

It doesn't *have* to be that way.

Wasp, please--don't take this the wrong way, but we're never going to so much as *consider* that.

Please don't bring it up again.

I know your feelings on the matter. I do. And I understand everyone's concerns, but something has come up.

Something that proves my recovery from *The Hunger* is not a fluke--that I'm not an isolated case.

I found it earlier today, grandfathers.

He's like Miss Wasp--he's nice. He hasn't tried to bite me once.

Do I know any of you? I remember... I *think* I remember...

Bring it here, son.

Be careful.

Hawkeye?

My God...

Meanwhile, out in deep space...

Fabian **Cortez**, my *father*, was a great man!

A man with VISION!

He would often speak to me of the vast world that lay around us, *untouched* and *unspoiled*. He believed in the *potential* of this society.

My father believed we could reestablish our dominance over this planet! *I* believe we can do much more than we are.

I believe we can start to *live* instead of merely trying to *survive!*

I've lost faith in our *"warrior king"* who's never fought in a war! I see a man who lives in fear--fear of the past--fear of the future.

I don't see a king! I see an *old man*, losing his mind--slowly rotting away to nothing-- taking *us* with him!

I call for a new direction, new ideas--new *leadership!*

Cortez!

Cortez!

Cortez!

Cortez!

Later that night.

Aboard Asteroid M, the quarters of Black Panther and his wife...

Elsewhere...

Just a few more--

What is this monitor saying? There's a *breach*? How often does that happen?

It happens from time to time. A hatch opening isn't such a big deal if we're not out in space. I usually *ignore* it.

I guess you could go check it out if you're really worried...

Hmm.

PANTHER!

Oh, God...

Oh, God...

He can't die--Wasp, please--don't let him die.

He's going to. He--

There's only one way to stop it.

What do you--oh, God-- oh, *no.*

CHOMP!

Oh, God--the *taste.* It was the only way. I had to do it.

The taste-- oh, so *good*-- the taste-- I--

Ugh. *Pain--it hurts!*

The hunger!

No! No-- *Please!!* *Stay back!*

Irk!

URRANN!

Well...

Hello.

Leave my... leave my wife *alone.*

If you have to eat someone-- help me eat *him.*

You're the boss.

I think my hunger is gone already... seemed like it took longer last time. Weird.

How about you? How do you feel?

I don't know... the pain is gone, but I don't know if it's gone away or if I've just gotten *used* to it.

Forge--I think his hunger is gone too. I'd keep an eye on him just to be safe--but I think we can be released now.

It's not going to be that simple. Malcolm Cortez has taken over the colony--it's taken everything I've got to keep him from trying to execute you both.

He keeps saying he wants to end the zombie plague forever... it's hard for people to argue with him.

And everyone is just ignoring the fact that it was an attack *he* ordered that caused everything that's happened with T'Challa and me?

Unless you think you can convince him to prosecute himself-- that's a losing argument.

I'm sorry, Wasp. There's very little I can do at this point.

ARRG!

KRAKK!

Huh.

Broke a finger... that'll need to be repaired.

Just do whatever you can, Forge.

Saying your goodbyes?

Yes.

Just because I'm not standing in your way doesn't mean I agree with you.

Fair enough.

All that matters is that by tomorrow morning the threat of the zombie plague will be gone forever.

Make sure you deliver your new friend Hawkeye to us in the morning as well.

I know the deal.

He'll be there-- they'll *all* be there. It's for the good of mankind... I get it.

I just don't know how I'll ever look my grandson in the eyes again.

Later that night.

It's weird, I don't... I'm not tired. I'm not hungry... I'm just... numb.

You get used to that. It was weird at first for me, too... not sleeping, never getting tired. You'd be surprised how much you can get done now.

GETTING IT DONE!

What the--?!

Hawkeye, keep it down!

Sorry. I'll be good.

Why did you have to bring him, again, Reynolds?

He cries if I leave him alone.

Almost done.

There.

You guys coming, or what?

So, no hunger? You're pretty much back to normal?

Normal? No. But the hunger is gone. There are differences--I feel different, but my mind is intact, that's what is important.

Thank you for the bandage... I was having trouble keeping my insides *inside*.

You'll need to take Hawkeye with you. You, him and Wasp will need to lie low... hide out in the city.

We'll send a signal when Cortez has been dealt with... I just don't see anyone allowing him to lead for too long.

I doubt it will be more than a month or two.

Okay, understood. We'll be on the lookout. We'll spend the time looking for any supplies we could use. The time won't be wasted.

C'mon... you have to follow me.

Are we going for a ride?

Janet, you be careful.

Will do. I'll be back to be your guinea pig before you know it, Reynolds. Don't worry about me.

I'm afraid I can't avoid that.

Make sure--

You don't even have to say it. I'll keep an eye on K'Shamba and Hendricks. They'll be fine.

K'Shamba's going to be so scared without me. I just wish I could see him before I go.

Maybe I can help with that.

Well, your own grandson has made his choice. Let's see what everyone else has to say.

PEOPLE OF NEW WAKANDA-- I HAVE AN ANNOUNCEMENT TO MAKE!

WRAMM!!

GRRUNNCH!

NO!

VZAPP!!

VPP!

Listen to yourself, Giant Man... listen to what you're saying! For God's sake, man--have you lost your mind?!

I've been traveling out in space for forty years-- eating and killing, devouring everything in sight...only to learn I'd be coming back here, to Earth... a place where I can't hide what I once was--can't forget it, the evidence is right here--all around us.

We were *heroes.*

And we return to find living people here! With *families!* We can't do this again! We just can't!

I won't let you!

Huh...

Colonel America would be proud.

...

Someone kill this little twit.

Kinda always knew it would come to this eventually, Pete.

What the--?!

Leave him alone!

What's wrong with you people?! Can't you see he's *right*?!

Go! Get inside-- we'll hold them off if they come after you.

Run!

Hey-- what's going on?

Huh? What's that?

It's me--Reynolds-- I'm transmitting to you through Hawkeye's robot body.

What?

Can you get the Asteroid into orbit? Once the people are on, can you get them out of here?

Then they can just fly up and get us in space. I think we're safer here-- I've been working on something.

Watch them--see if you can steer their fight to the edge of New Wakanda... the minute they cross out of the settlement, signal me through Hawkeye.

Will do.

WASP--I'M GOING TO NEED YOUR HELP!

C'mon--we gotta push them out of the settlement.

I'll do my best!

HEY!!

Hunger-- fading.

It's about time. I didn't think I could hold you back a second longer.

Off me!

Crap.

Get a hold of yourselves! This accomplishes *nothing!*

WRAMM!

That's as close as we're going to get. Whatever it is you're going to do, Reynolds--

--do it now!!

Okay, here goes.

Pray this works!

VMMNNMNMMMNMMNMMNMNMMMMMMMMNNNN!!

I want to do this!

Why bother with your pathetic energy blasts? I can't even *feel* them.

It makes *me* feel better!

Plus--it's a distraction!

Huh?

Spider-Man, you still with us?!

Wow.

Heh. Now we get to find out who's inside.

Quickly-- while he's stunned-- hold him in place!

I'll do what I can-- just make this quick!

Can't-- move!

Can't-- think!

Nice job! But, Luke--I gotta say, you really look like crap.

I don't know how that's possible, I just lost like eighty pounds!

THUD

Come here, Wasp--let's get you patched up.

Hey!
Hey!

Who are you? How did you build that?

I hate to break it to you, Tony--but the doors at Stark International aren't locked anymore.

I've had *forty years* to improve upon everything you've ever done.

Forge?! I didn't even know you were still *alive*.

I am--at least for a little while longer.

Also, you're never going to get through that force field--so you might as well give up.

Whatever-- he may be right. However, killing them isn't why we came back to Earth.

Come on.

Here it is.

The Baxter Building, Former Home of the Fantastic Four.

Nice place.

Well, as I recall, we did kind of make a mess of things before we left the planet.

Fan out-- we need to find this gateway Reed built soon.

I'm starting to forget the taste of--

What are we going to do with *him*?

Keep him drugged and unconscious for as long as we possibly can in hopes that we figure something out.

If he wakes up-- turns into the Hulk... those restraints won't do a thing.

What about you, T'Challa? Do you feel anything?

No, nothing. It's like it didn't even happen. I can *see* it--but I can't *feel* it.

I'm not feeling *this* either--but if someone could get me reattached to my body, it'd be nice to--

Right away--sorry, Mrs. Wasp.

Thanks, Reynolds-- and how many times do I have to tell you? It's most certainly *Ms.* Wasp *these* days.

And you can call me *Janet.* I've known you longer than I knew my ex-husband...

We're in the middle of a crisis here, people. When did you think it would be a good time to inform your *leader* of what's going on?

Our future is in jeopardy-- I need to be informed!

Get him *out* of here!

You know as well as I do that none of us will survive this if we don't work together. So whatever it is you have against me--I suggest you get over it for the time being.

He's right-- we'll need everyone if we're going to survive.

Well--not everyone. Working with your kind is an accident waiting to happen!

Malcolm, they've already risked their lives to save us--and look-- they're *not* attacking us.

We're not going to be able to do this without *their kind!*

...

Very well...

Later...

Just plug me up--I don't need legs to get around. You're just wasting time.

Where did these come from exactly?

The Wasp had gone through quite a few bodies before we got to the current model. These are leftovers.

It was a simple matter to rig them up so you could control them.

I can do a little better than that.

So you guys have been living here this whole time?

We stayed in orbit for a few years, making sure it was safe down on the surface. Then yes, we returned here.

It hasn't always been great-- but we've survived.

You've been living life. I miss life.

I miss smells... I miss food...

I miss a lot of things...

I'm sorry, he-- he wanted to see you.

Please, come. Don't be afraid, K'Shamba. You have nothing to fear from me.

I'm not afraid. I'm--

Are-- are you *dead*?

Do I sound dead to you?

No...but you *look* dead.

What have I told you in your studies? Looks can be deceiving... never judge anything by looks alone.

I am still your grandfather.

Well, everyone is scared. They're all saying that we're going to die.

If I die, I don't want to stay dead like Mom and Dad-- I want to come back just like *you*.

What can the two of you tell us about your group? Any information would be useful.

Why are they here? Why have they come back?

The same reason we went everywhere else in the galaxy: for more *food*...

They're looking for a place that has it.

Then why *here*? They had to know that even if there were survivors here--it wouldn't be *enough*.

There's a device here-- something Reed developed when this all started. The thing the Fantastic Four used to travel to another dimension.

What? Why are you *smiling*?

Follow me. There's something I'd like to show you.

Oh, God-- you've got it *here?*

I anticipated this. I thought you might one day return. I sought this machine out--mostly in order to keep it out of your hands.

At the same time, I wanted to give us the ability to escape this living hell-- but I've failed. I've checked and rechecked the machine, and while nothing seems to be wrong with it--it simply doesn't *work.*

You brought it *here?!*

You don't understand. They came here for that machine--all the way here, from the edge of the *known universe*--just for *that.*

They will stop at *nothing* until they have it. They have time on their side--they can figure out a way to get past your force field.

You *will* eventually have to fight them!

We can't face them like this--we don't have the strength or the numbers needed to fight them off.

Uh...I may be able to help with that second part.

Out on our expeditions into the city we found something--a brain. Well, *part* of a brain, really.

It was still functioning--at least, partially. It was *amazing*-- so we kept it.

I was studying it--trying to determine a way to see how well it was functioning-- a way to test it...

...when, suddenly, an opportunity presented itself.

I was shocked, really. I couldn't believe it had all worked. It was-- well, it was amazing.

The subject is an excellent fighter-- that part remained intact. Sadly, many other brain functions are impaired.

Still, I think you'll all be very impressed... once you get past the initial shock, that is.

T'Challa, this will probably be the hardest for you.

What? Why?

You'll see.

CLICK

T'Channa, *please*--don't you recognize me? It's *me*--your *father*...

This ends *here!* This ends *now!*

Son?!

WRAKK!!

No... this *isn't* your son--there's nothing left of your son in there. He died, his *brain died.* This is only his--his *body.*

But we found Colonel America's brain years ago--I swear I reported it to you-- maybe you just didn't feel it was important. It's been so long, I just--

When your son died, we-- we couldn't help but experiment, it was--

We--?!

Colonel-- don't you remember us?

You're beating on Panther--not saving the world-- what's with you?!

Whugh--

Wuh--

I--I forgot, I hadn't realized. My strength... and you...I'm sorry.

I'm sorry, old friend.

You are *not* forgiven-- but I'm sorry.

Fine-- *fine.*

If you can keep your hands off Reynolds and me until this is over I promise we'll settle this later.

If Giant Man and the rest are really here searching for the dimensional portal that Reed and the Fantastic Four used to leave this world--then we'd better get prepared.

It's not going to take them long to realize that we've got it here--and if we're not ready for them when they get here--we're *dead.*

We need to come up with a plan.

It's not working! She's too powerful!

Just keep it up--she's got to slip up sooner or later!

BLAGGG!

Whoa!

IRK!

I'm sick of all this useless fighting! Quit dancing around and let's kill all these jerks!

T'CHALLA!

Hank, you monster! You--

--monster!!

Oh, Janet-- how I've *missed* you over those long decades in space. Luckily...

Reynolds' Lab.

Janet, oh God--not you. Not you, Janet...

Oh, God...

You should have kept me sedated-- I was too smart for your restraints.

Big mistake.

Don't misunderstand me-- I'm not like the others. I don't *enjoy* this--I haven't accepted my fate.

I *hate* this-- I don't want to be doing this.

But the *hunger*-- I can feel it--it will bring out the Hulk. I've got seconds... minutes at most. If I eat you, it will calm me down.

I *have* to do this!

Please-- *no!*

Please-- be careful with the console--just don't--

CLICK

Oh, no...

VMMMMMM--

The force field--!

Oh, crap!

BREAK AWAY!

Go and *feast!* If they've got no one left to protect, this fight is over!

Move!

What's happening? What did I--?!

Are they getting *inside?!* Are the rest of them coming in? That's not what I wanted-- I *didn't!*

We've got to--

Oh, no-- it's too late! They're already inside!

Something's happening!

What is it?! What's going on?!

I noticed it, too.

The hunger is gone...

The horror *is* over.

Let that man go, Wolverine.

War's over, soldier--time for some *R & R*.

Just let him go.

Okay.

Th-thank you...

So... what now?

Gyukk Nakk, guh.

We stop what we've been doing, Iron Man--we change our ways. We help these people rebuild.

We can be heroes again.

We can--

Firelord, what'd you just say?

WRA-KOOM!!

You don't understand-- we don't want to fight you anymore.

It's *over*-- we're cured of the hunger. It's worn off--my wife was right, you were *all* right. We don't hunger for human flesh any longer.

So, uh...

Truce?

Hulk just wants to be left *alone!*

KLUKK!

VZAPP!

Firelord!

United we stand--

You will leave Hulk *alone!*

You will never bother Hulk again!

WRAMM!

KRRRRKK!

KRKKKKKK!

SPLLKKKKK!

Stop! Just stop!

Janet is gone-- I've got *nothing* now, nothing to live for.

If you have to eat someone-- eat *me*.

Don't try to stop him-- let him do this!

I *want* this!

Reynolds, we can't just let--

No time.

We... dear God...

...the things we did...

Hulk not hu--

Hulk feel funny...

I'm-I'm back. I'm Banner.

Ugh, you--

You have to kill me...

Later.

Ungh.

Oh, there you are.

It's about time.

Janet...?

What do *you* want?

I...I just thought we should talk.

I'm--I'm sorry for...for *everything*. I'm sorry about trying to kill you, I'm sorry if I hurt you. I'm sorry I left you...I'm sorry I allowed the hunger to completely take over.

I'm sorry for a lot of things.

I'm sorry about *Reynolds*.

Reynolds was...he--

Nobody knew him like I did. He was gentle and sweet, he cared so much about everyone around him, not just me. He was...

He was probably the greatest man I ever knew.

...

You always knew how to make me feel *small*.

And you always dealt with it in completely the wrong way.

I know why you're really here. Don't worry...I'm coming to your stupid meeting.

You wouldn't want to be late, right? You coming?

I'm right behind you.

here.

Forge?

What is this all about?

Giant-Man, you can start.

Thank you, Malcolm. As you all know, in the last few weeks, we've been working on repairing Reed's portal.

This community could find much-needed supplies in any number of dimensions, and frankly, the gene pool here isn't diverse enough to sustain life for more than a few more generations.

We're nearing extinction.

So, with the help of Malcolm and Forge--

Why isn't he here?

--we set out to repair the portal... and to our surprise, it was actually quite *easy.*

I suppose I should just come out with it, right now. It was easy because the only reason it wasn't working already...was *sabotage.*

What are you saying?!

I'm saying the only reason Forge couldn't get this thing working years ago is because I took a few key components *out.*

I grew up here-- I actually *like* it here. I don't even want to know what life was like with *"civilization."* This place is perfect--a manageable population, easy to rule, no outside threats, until *you* came...but we're fixing that... ...*right now.*

I'm getting rid of you-- especially *that* one. Do you have any idea how difficult it is to look at someone you've killed walking around-- talking?

And *yes,* Panther...I killed your son, *and* organized your attempted murder-- and when your grandson is old enough... ...I'm going to kill *him,* too.

You *fool*--you think I'll let you live another day after hearing this?! Why are you saying all this-- why show your hand?!

Because I *can.*

Finally... *Gone.*

Where are they?! Where did they go?!

What did you do? Where did you send them?!

All that matters is they're gone! They were an accident waiting to happen--our extinction *guaranteed!*

Can't you see this *needed* to happen?!

No! They were our friends--they were going to help us!

We have to get them back!

HARD TO BELIEVE WE'VE HIT THE FINISH LINE FOR THIS, THE SECOND MARVEL ZOMBIES MINI-SERIES, ALREADY. IT SEEMS LIKE JUST YESTERDAY I WAS SITTING DOWN TRYING TO FIGURE OUT HOW TO TURN THIS KOOKY IDEA INTO A STORY. I'D LIKE TO THANK SEAN, JUNE, RUS, RANDY, ARTHUR, BILL, LAUREN, NICOLE, JOHN AND RALPH FOR ALL THEIR CONTRIBUTIONS ON THE TWO MINI-SERIES. I'D ALSO LIKE TO THANK ALL OF YOU, EACH AND EVERY ONE OF YOU, FOR PURCHASING THIS. I HOPE YOU FEEL THE SECOND STORY LIVED UP TO THE FIRST--AND DON'T FORGET...THERE WAS A QUESTION MARK BEHIND "THE END" ON THAT LAST PAGE.

—ROBERT

CIVIL WAR #1 Variant cover by Michael Turner

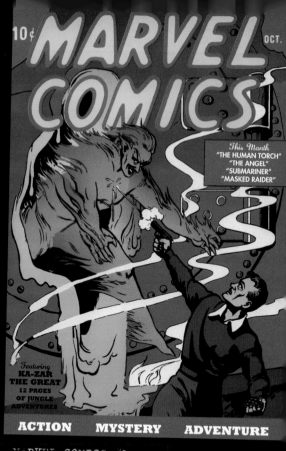

MARVEL COMICS #1 cover by Frank Paul

TALES OF SUSPENSE #39 cover by Jack Kirby

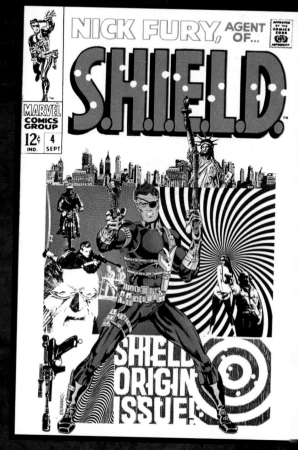

S.H.I.E.L.D. #4 cover by Jim Steranko

SILVER SURFER #4 cover by John Buscema

ROBERT KIRKMAN

SEAN PHILLIPS

ROBERT KIRKMAN

CURRENTLY WRITING: *Marvel Zombies 2, Ultimate X-Men*, Marvel; *Walking Dead, Invincible*, Image
ZOMBIE CRED: *Marvel Zombies #1-5, Dead Days* one-shot, *Marvel Zombies 2 #1-5*
FAVORITE ZOMBIE MOVIE: *Day of the Dead*... but *Shaun of the Dead* is a close second.
FAVORITE SUYDAM ZOMBIE COVER: *Marvel Zombies #4*, the *X-Men #1* cover. Love that cover to *Dead Days*, though.
FAVORITE COVER NOT YET ZOMBIEFIED: *New Mutants #82*, the first appearance of Cable.
FAVORITE MARVEL ZOMBIE MOMENT: The opening scene of *Marvel Zombies 2* is my current favorite. Sean (Phillips) really knocked that one out of the park.

WHICH MARVEL ZOMBIE WOULD YOU MOST WANT TO BE: Sleepwalker
IF YOU WERE A ZOMBIE, WHO WOULD YOU MOST WANT TO EAT: Mayor McCheese... I'd make a crappy zombie.

SEAN PHILLIPS

CURRENTLY DRAWING: *Marvel Zombies 2, Criminal*
ZOMBIE CRED: *Marvel Zombies #1-5, Marvel Zombies/Army of Darkness #4-5, Dead Days* one-shot, *Marvel Zombies 2 #1-5*
FAVORITE ZOMBIE MOVIE: *Shaun of the Dead*
FAVORITE SUYDAM ZOMBIE COVER: *Marvel Zombies HC*, fifth printing, featuring *Mary Jane #2*
FAVORITE MARVEL ZOMBIE MOMENT: Getting that royalty check.
WHICH MARVEL ZOMBIE WOULD YOU MOST WANT TO BE: Hawkeye
IF YOU WERE A ZOMBIE, WHO WOULD YOU MOST WANT TO EAT: No one. I'm a vegetarian!